# *Papercutting*
# PATTERN BOOK

## Claudia Hopf

STACKPOLE
BOOKS

*To papercutters the world over—*
*those who inspired us in the past,*
*those working today,*
*and those who will discover the art*

Copyright ©2010 by Stackpole Books

Published by
STACKPOLE BOOKS
5067 Ritter Road
Mechanicsburg, PA 17055
www.stackpolebooks.com

Printed in the United States of America

10  9  8  7  6  5  4  3  2  1

FIRST EDITION

Cover design by Tessa J. Sweigert

**Library of Congress Cataloging-in-Publication Data**

Hopf, Claudia.
    Papercutting pattern book / Claudia Hopf. — 1st ed.
        p. cm.
    ISBN-13: 978-0-8117-0575-2 (pbk.)
    ISBN-10: 0-8117-0575-7 (pbk.)
    1. Paper work. 2. Cut-out craft. I. Title.
    TT870.H658 2010
    745.54—dc22
                                2010001780

# *Papercutting*
## PATTERN BOOK

0  11557 00575  2

# Contents

# Introduction

My love affair with papercutting began in the 1960s when I first saw an intricate 1810 birth certificate *scherenschnitte* at Landis Valley Museum in Lancaster, Pennsylvania. *Scherenschnitte* is the term for papercutting in the Pennsylvania Dutch dialect. After seeing this amazing piece, I sought out other papercuttings. The collection at Landis also included children's naïve cuttings. These charming examples were cut from any paper available—old ledgers, newspapers, letters, wallpapers, and small bits of colored paper.

I began learning by trying these simpler designs. I started on white paper and then moved on to black. I mounted the designs on wallpapers and fabrics. As I gained confidence, I moved on to more complex cuttings.

The next step I took was antiquing the paper. First I tried tea to stain the surface of white paper, but I found the color to be too pink. I then tried using instant coffee. The result proved to be much closer in simulating the foxing, or yellowish brown stains, found on old paper. To add dimension, I pin-pricked small interior spaces, such as facial features, hair, clothing, veins in leaves, and flower petals.

Then I began painting my cuttings with a basic color palette. I mainly used dark colors, but through the years I added brighter hues. Experimenting with papers, I used anything that had interesting color and texture. I found that flower and plant catalogs have wonderful floral illustrations printed on smooth, thin paper. When these are folded and cut, they produce exciting marble effects.

At first, my designs were based on Pennsylvania Dutch *scherenschnitte*. I soon discovered, however, that artistic papercutting has been practiced for centuries in many cultures around the world. I learned more about the varieties of cutting in Switzerland, Germany, Poland, and China, and I added these influences to my craft.

My subjects for cutting include birds, animals, flowers, garden designs, and scenic images with people. Botanicals especially lend themselves to perfect outline design and can be done in black silhouette or white with colorful painting. I began to paint more realistic images on the cuttings when customers asked me to do portraits of their dogs and cats. Elaborate Biblical subjects have also been popular, especially the Peaceable Kingdom, Noah's Ark, and Adam and Eve in the Garden of Eden.

## ABOUT THE PATTERNS

In this book, you will find a nice variety of papercutting patterns. They are all my own original designs, although some are inspired by other papercutting traditions. The patterns can be reduced or enlarged. The larger the design, the easier it is to cut. Smaller designs, obviously, are more intricate and challenging. The dots on the patterns indicate areas where you may punch holes with a pin.

After you gain more experience, try new ideas. It can be fun to add insects or small animals to botanicals—a bumblebee to a flower, a frog under a thicket of ferns, or a chipmunk next to a tree. Doing this gives the design visual appeal and adds your own personal touch. You can use parts of patterns and add them to others if you wish.

Below are the general needs and steps for papercutting. For more complete information on the craft, including a variety of designs by other practitioners from various countries, see my book *Papercutting: Tips, Tools, and Techniques for Learning the Craft*.

## TOOLS AND MATERIALS

Papercutting requires no expensive tools. Essentially, all you need is a good pair of sharp iris scissors. If you want to cut heavier papers, you will need a craft knife and a self-healing backmat. Have a pin handy, too, for punching small holes when the design calls for it.

Twenty-pound laid paper is the best type to use with iris scissors. White is preferred if you plan to stain or paint on the paper. Any paper can be used, however. You may want to experiment with magazines, calendars, rice paper, and old antique paper. You can photocopy the patterns from the book if you wish, but you may want to trace them and transfer them to paper. For tracing, you will need tracing paper, a soft lead pencil, double-sided transparent tape, and a burnishing tool or spoon.

For staining, you will need a sponge, water, instant coffee, soft tissues, and paper towels. For painting, you will need a #2 or #3 sable brush and the following watercolor paints: cadmium yellow, yellow ochre, cadmium red, alizarin crimson, Prussian blue, burnt sienna, permanent white, and lamp black. For mounting, I recommend black velour paper and an acid-free glue stick.

## TRACING AND TRANSFERRING THE PATTERN

To make cuttings of the patterns in this book, you can simply photocopy them onto the paper you wish to use. If you decide to go this route, you are free to disregard this section. In some cases, however, you may not be able to load the paper you want to use into a copier, so you will have to trace the design from the book and transfer it to the paper following these steps.

Place a piece of tracing paper over the design. Be sure the tracing paper is secure by fastening double-sided tape at the top corners. Using a soft lead pencil, trace the design. Then place the tracing facedown on the paper to be cut. Secure the tracing with double-sided tape at the top corners. Rub over the lines with a burnishing tool or the edge of a spoon to transfer all the pencil lines onto the paper. Lift the tracing paper to see if all has been adequately transferred. You may need to fill in some lines.

## CUTTING

Begin by cutting away the inside areas first, starting at the center and working outward. First, open the scissors slightly and poke a hole in the first center area to be cut. Keeping the scissors in place, make small snips to the edges, then cut along the line until the piece falls away. Do not tear it away. Continue in the same fashion for all the pieces to be cut out. Cut the outside edges last. This allows you to grasp the paper easier while cutting away the inside pieces.

Here are some tips for cutting.

- To avoid raised edges on the paper, hold the scissors perpendicular to the paper while cutting. This will give you a smooth cut.
- For better control, keep your cutting hand stationary while the other hand moves the paper around the blade.
- To keep from overcutting, cut on the tips of the blades, completely closing them with each cut.

- To avoid tears, always completely close the scissors before you withdraw them.
- If you find the paper is binding the scissors when you are cutting from the top surface, withdraw the scissors and cut from beneath the paper. This will help you cut easier.

## FOLDED DESIGNS

This book includes a variety of folded patterns for symmetrical designs. You will need to transfer the design by tracing, so follow the steps above. To transfer, fold your paper in half and place the dotted-line side of the pattern against the fold. After the design is transferred to the paper, you will be cutting two layers.

## ANTIQUING, PAINTING, AND MOUNTING

To give your cutting an antique look, lay the finished piece on a paper towel with the penciled side down. Wet a sponge with warm water and squeeze into a small dish of instant coffee crystals. The crystals will melt into a thin paste. Using the sponge, dab the paste over the cutting evenly. Remove the moisture from the cutting with a soft tissue and let it dry. Press the cutting under a flat, clear surface, such as a piece of glass. Make sure no edges are folded under. Add weight to the glass; a heavy book is handy for this purpose.

Painting the cutting is a craft in itself and something that you will develop with practice. Watercolor paints are recommended, with suggested colors listed above. First, paint the base color; then let it dry and press. Next, overlay darker shades followed by the lighter ones. Finish by painting the white highlights.

For mounting, I use black velour paper for a dramatic contrast. You may prefer a softer brown or white for background paper. Adhere the design with an acid-free glue stick. Apply a few dabs along the center back of the cutting and then press under glass.

Remember to sign and date the cutting for reference.

# Floral

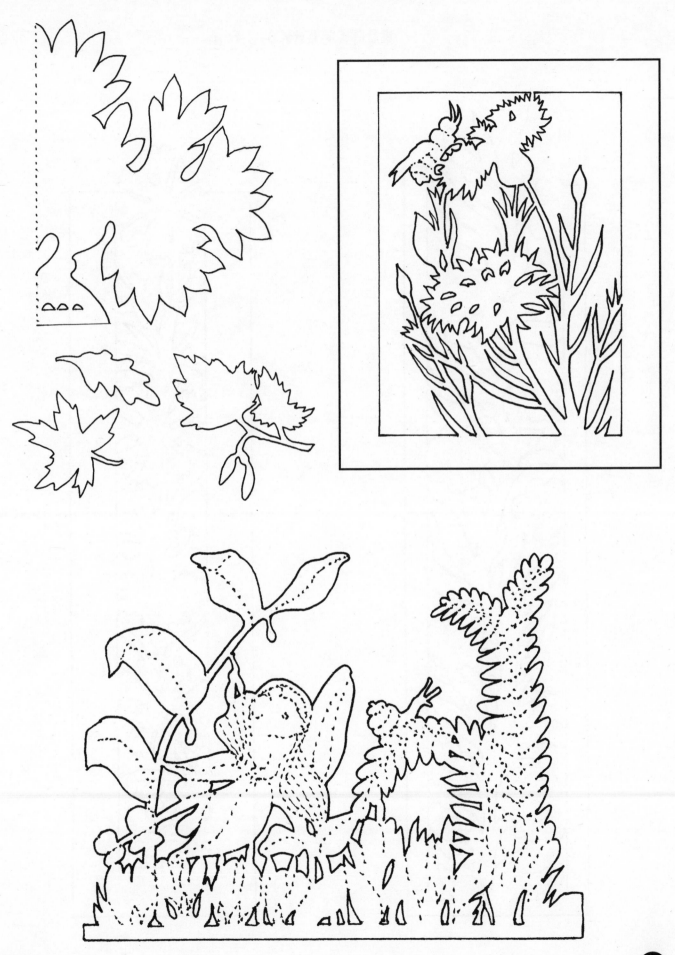

*Floral*

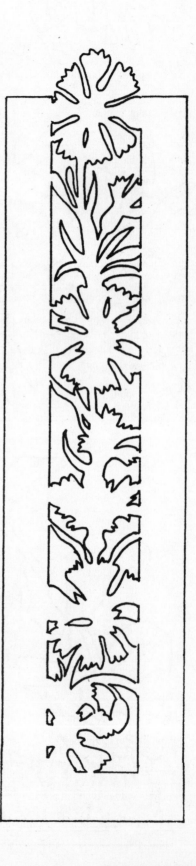

*Floral*

**Chicory**

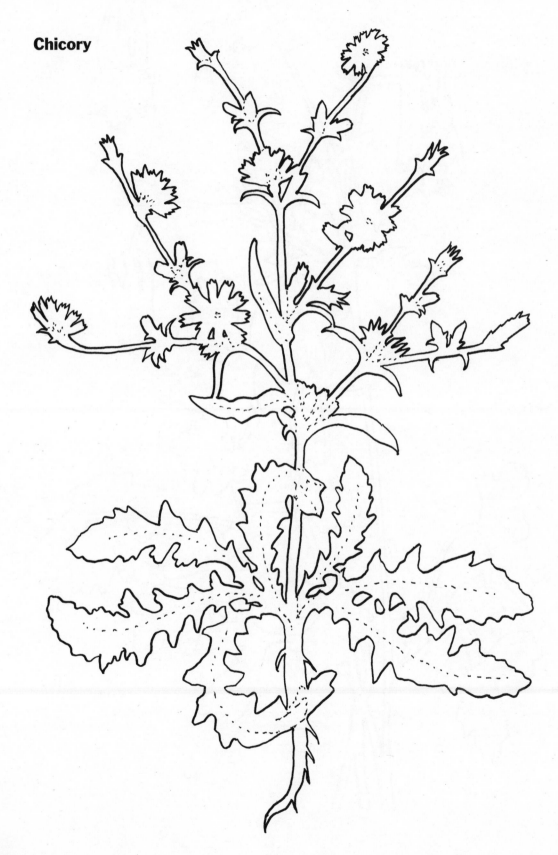

**Columbine**

**Iris**

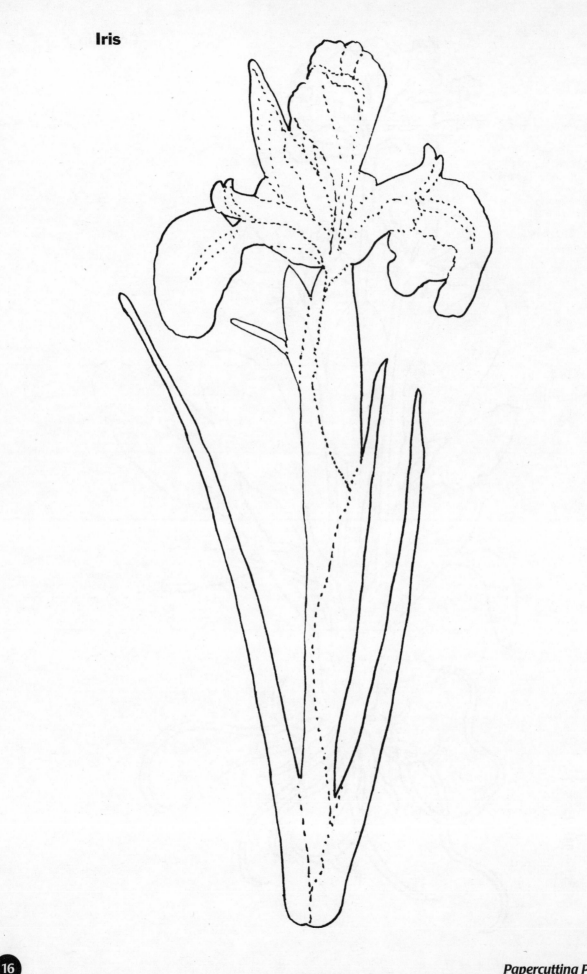

**Lavender**

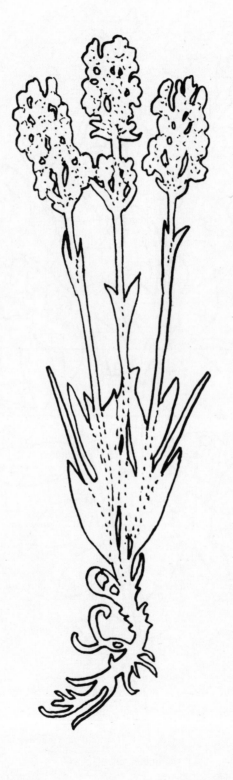

# Potentilla

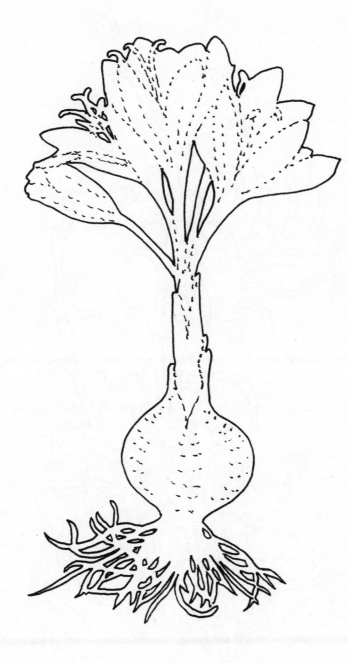

**Strawflower**

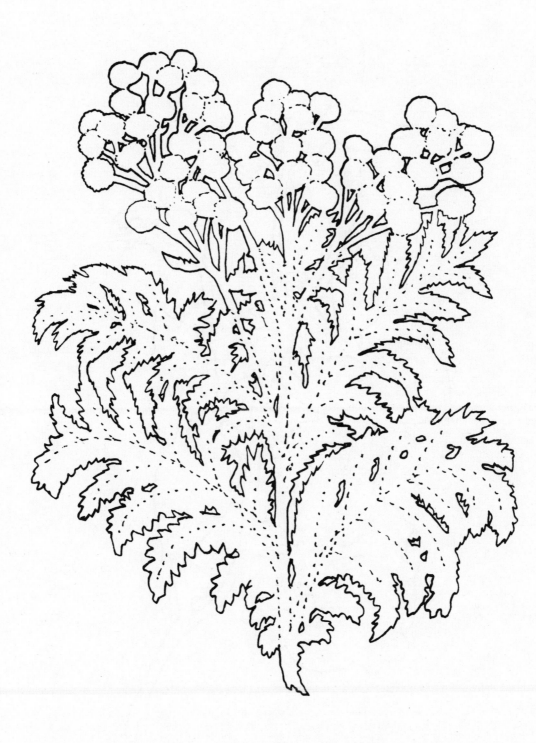

**Tea Rose**

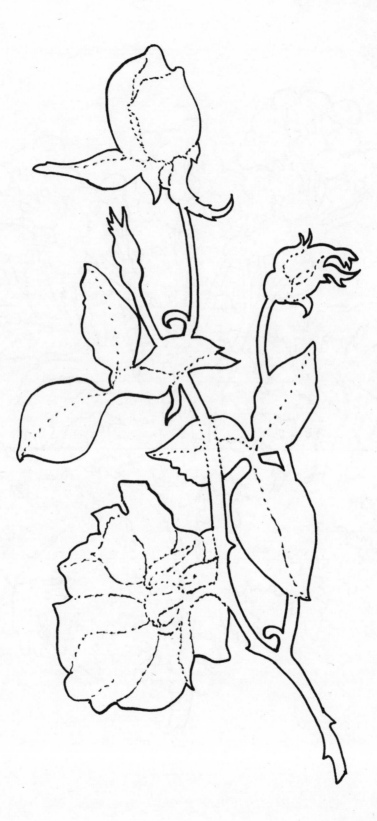

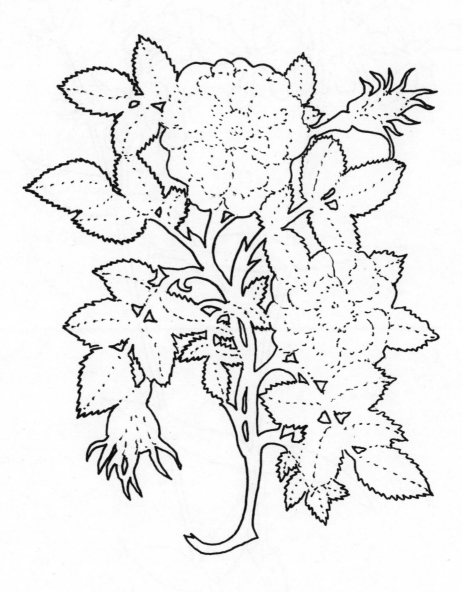

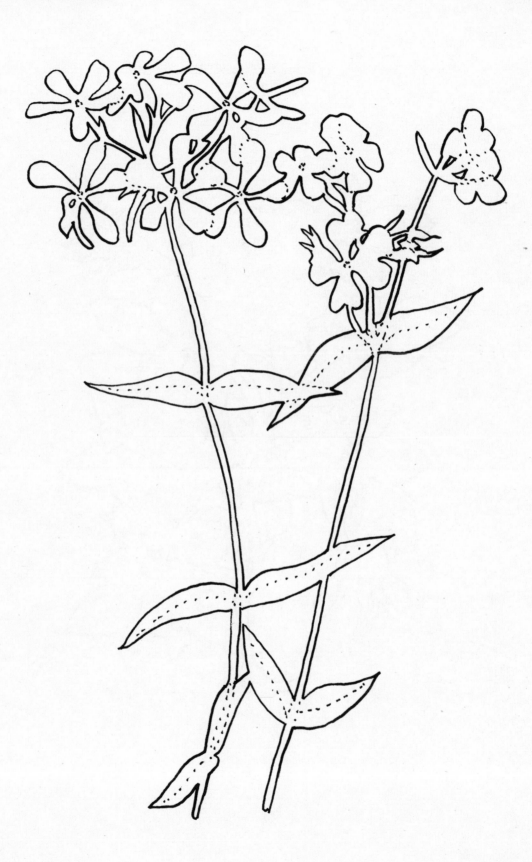

# Cats

# Dogs

**Fox and Grapes (Aesop fable)**

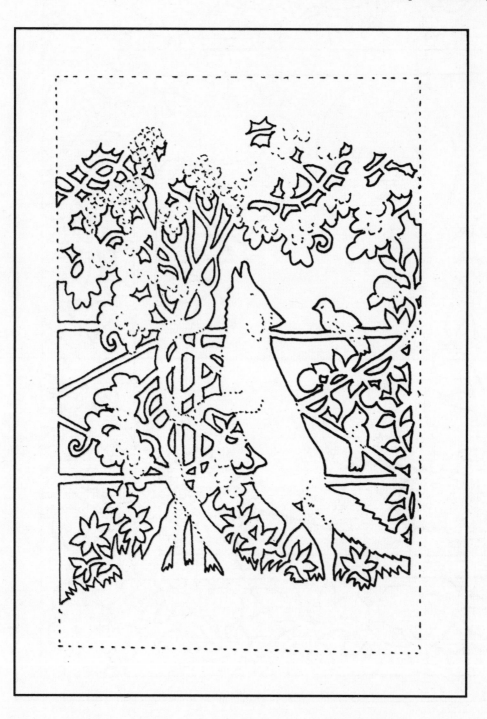

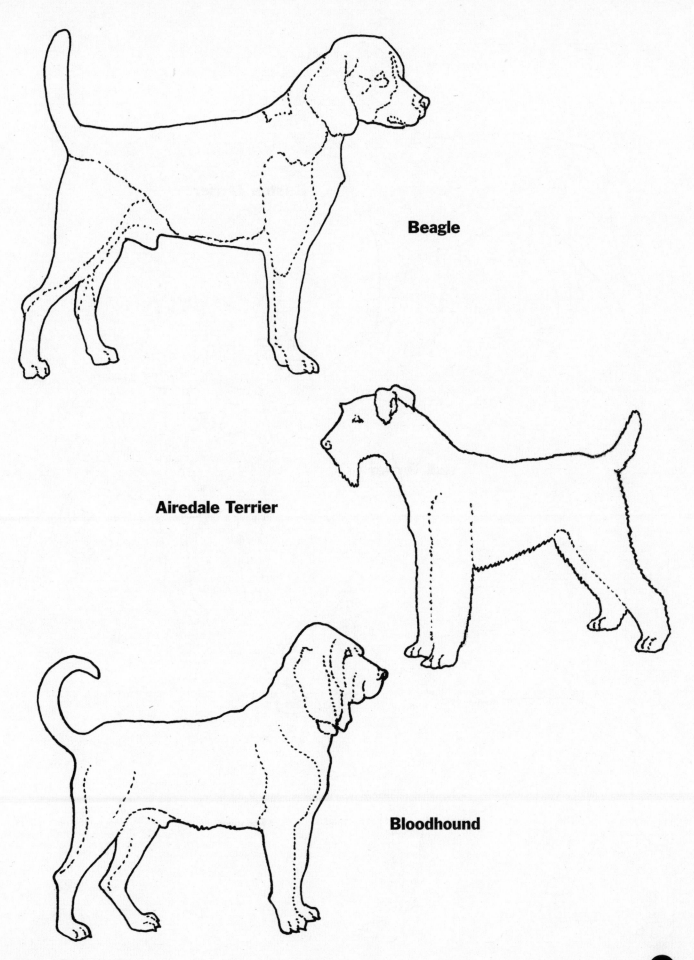

**Beagle**

**Airedale Terrier**

**Bloodhound**

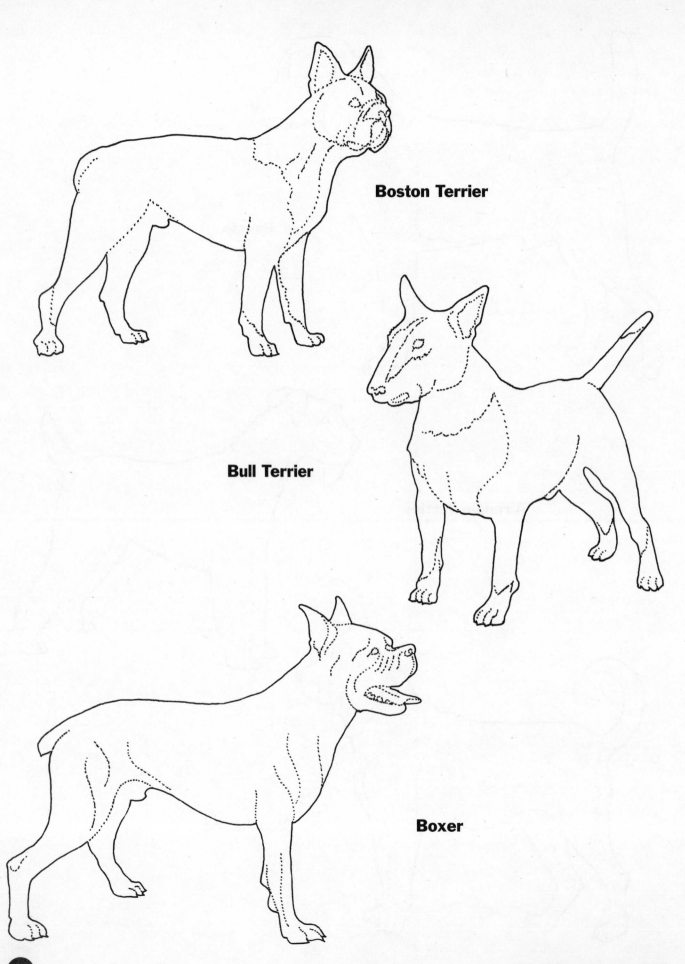

**Boston Terrier**

**Bull Terrier**

**Boxer**

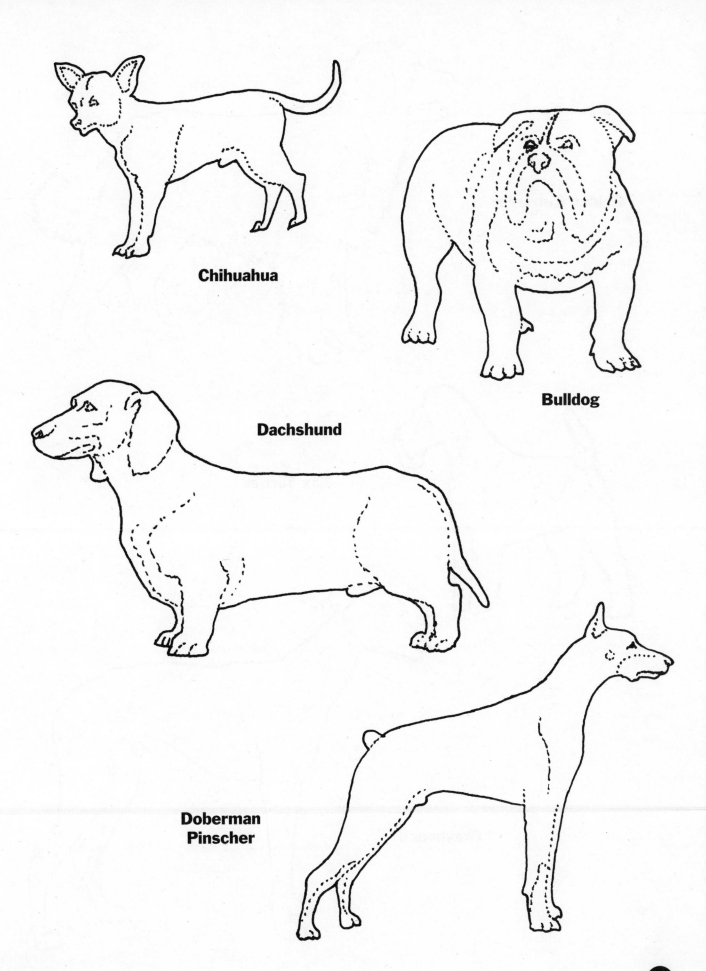

**Chihuahua**

**Bulldog**

**Dachshund**

**Doberman Pinscher**

**Golden Retriever**

**Fox Terrier**

**Greyhound**

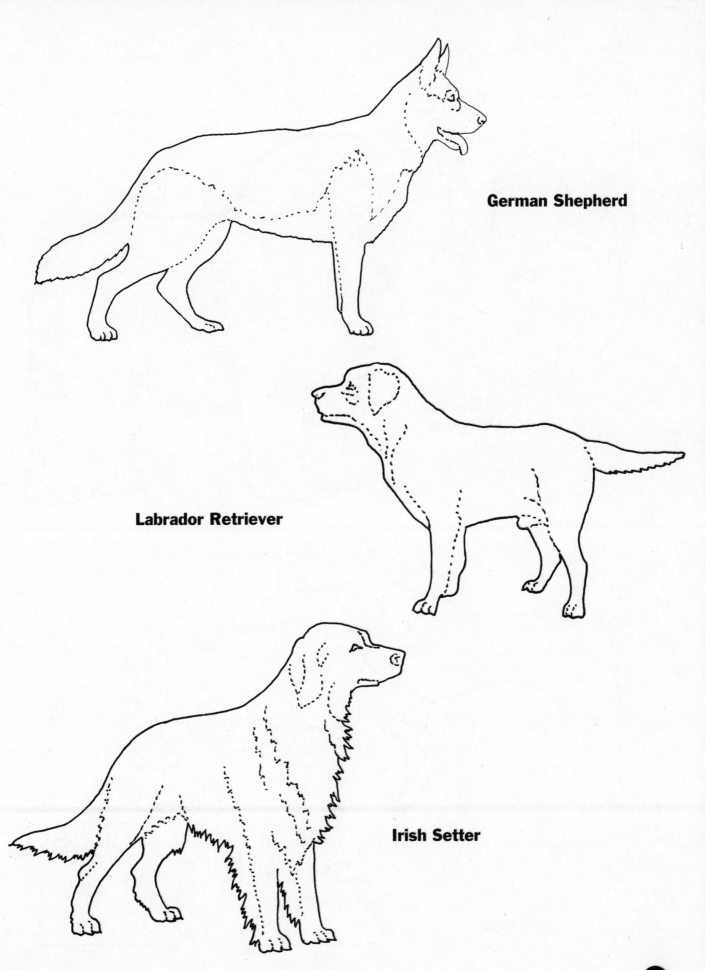

**German Shepherd**

**Labrador Retriever**

**Irish Setter**

Pug

Old English
Sheepdog

Pointer

Poodle

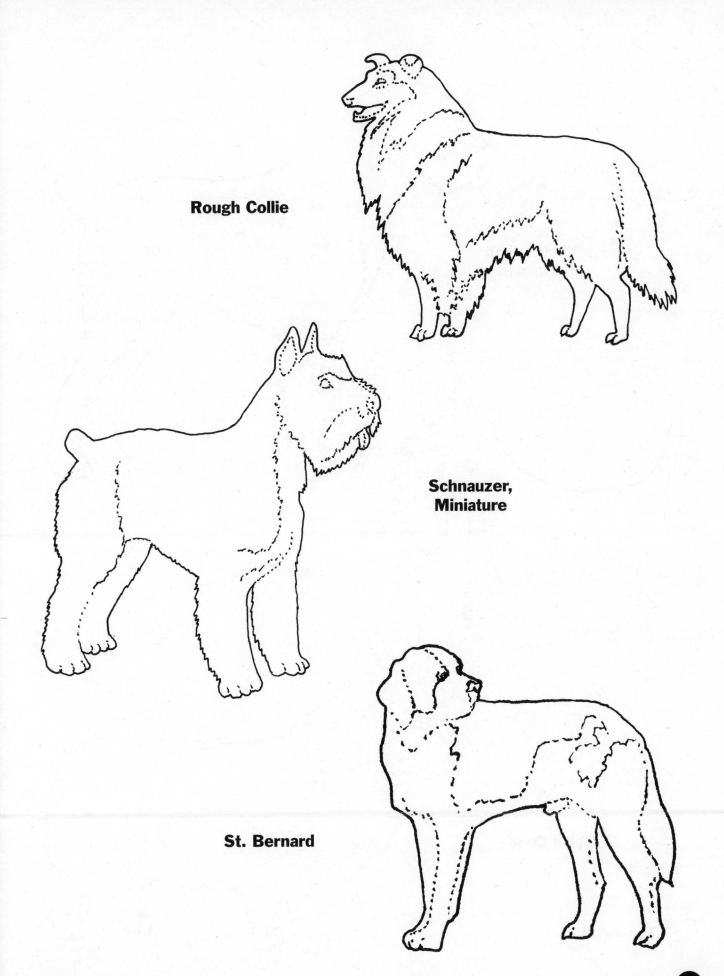

**Rough Collie**

**Schnauzer, Miniature**

**St. Bernard**

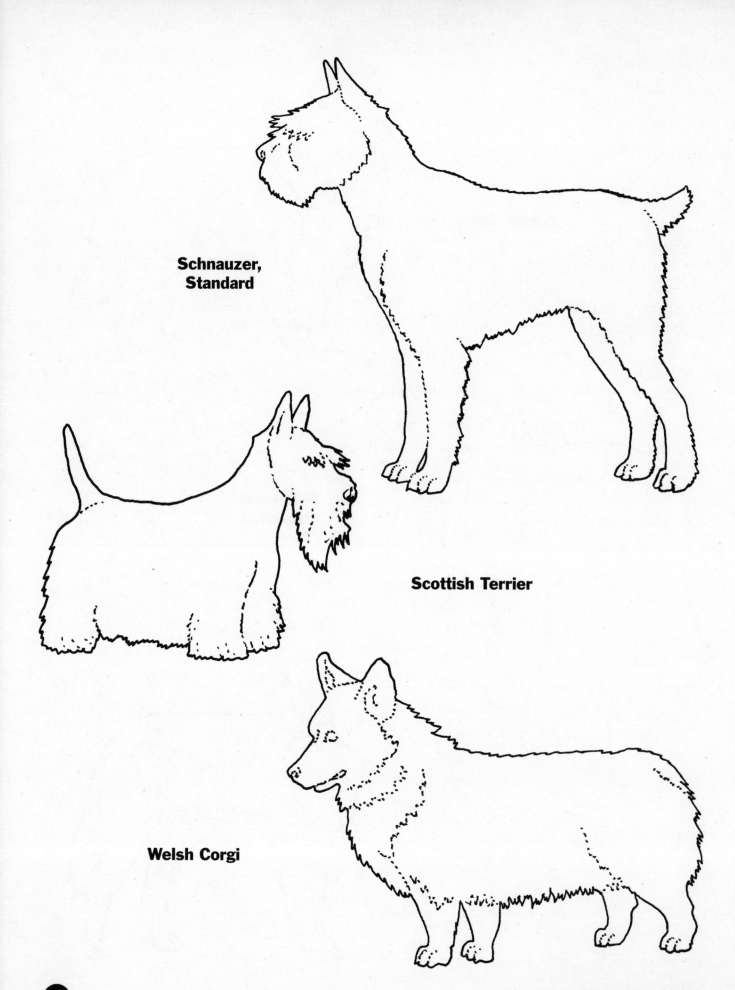

**Schnauzer, Standard**

**Scottish Terrier**

**Welsh Corgi**

# Birds

**Chickadee**

**Hummingbird**

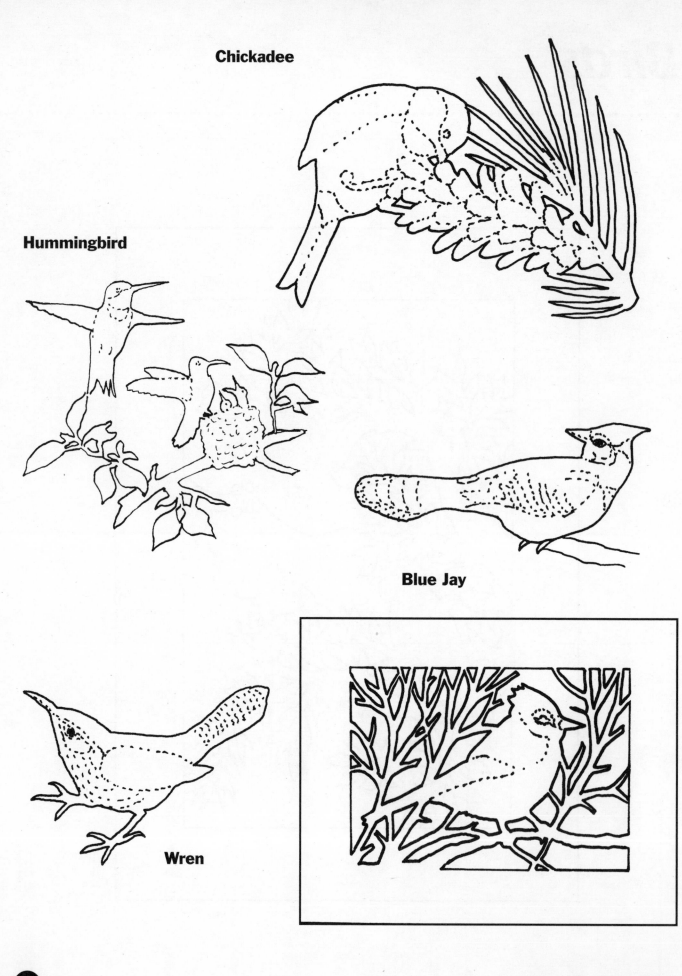

**Blue Jay**

**Wren**

**Great Blue Heron**

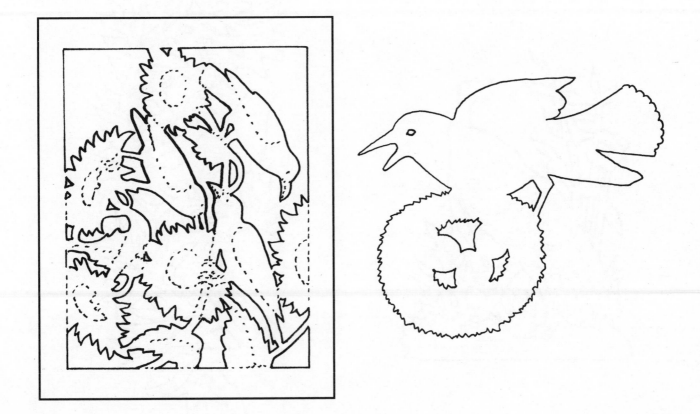

# Wild Animals

**Tortoise and the Hare**

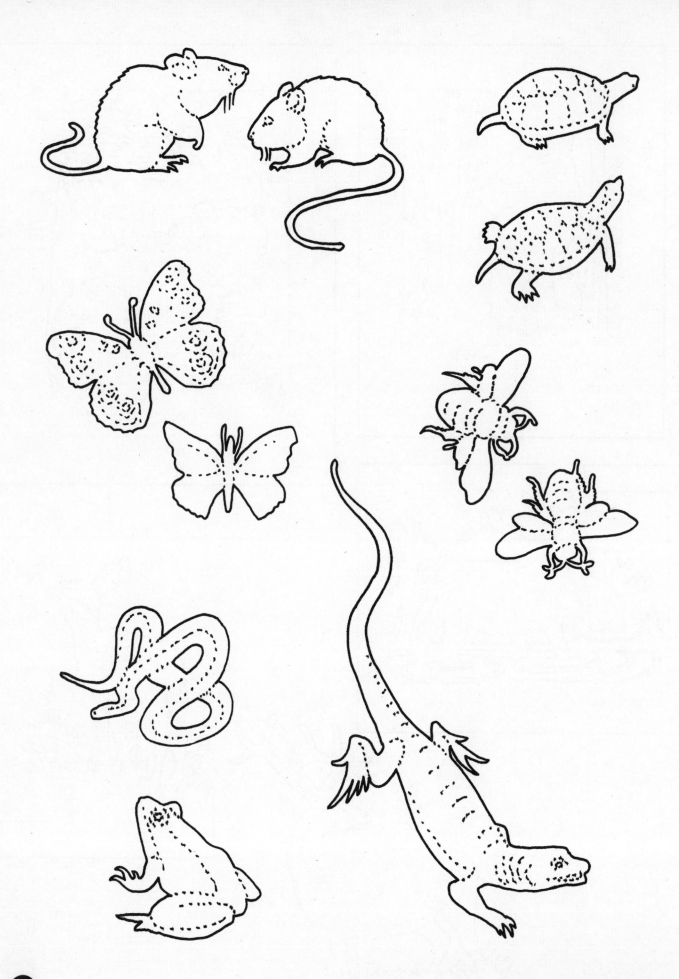

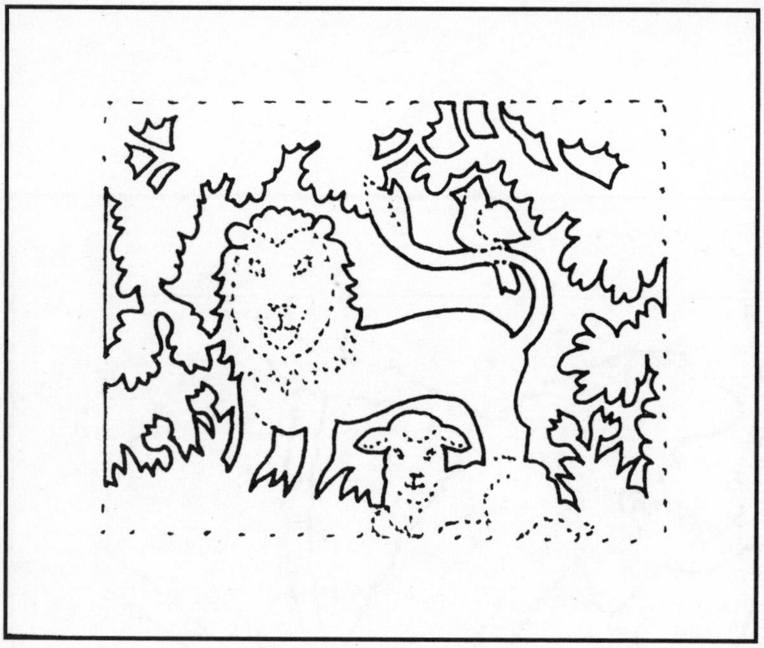

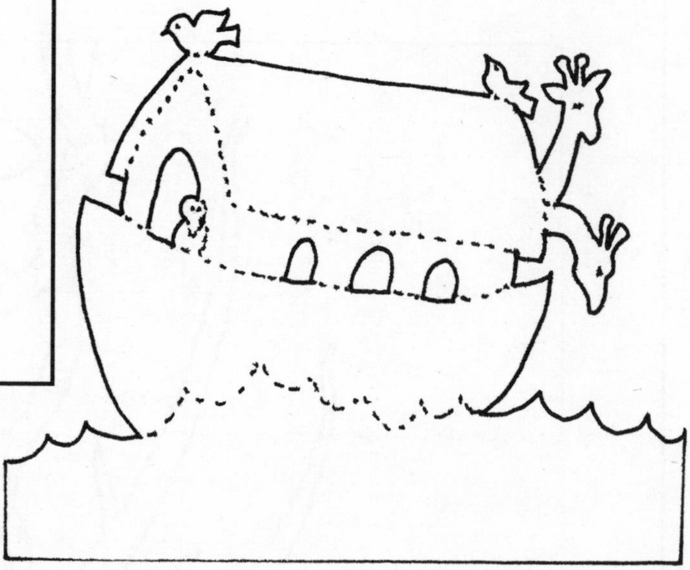

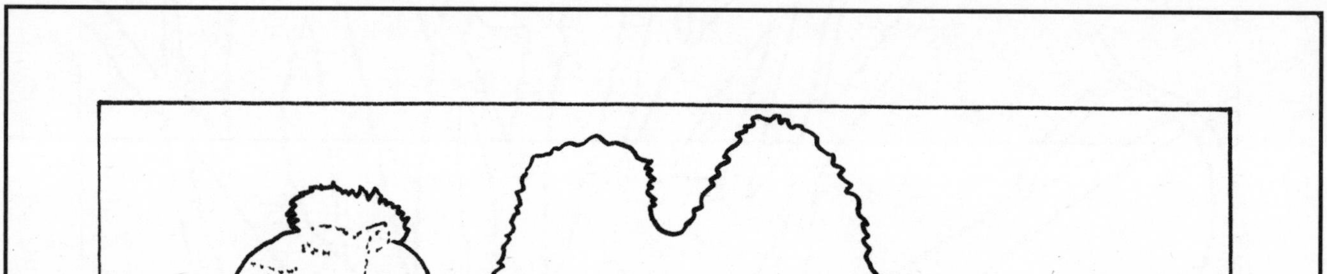

# Farm Animals

*Farm Animals*

## Bremen Town Musicians

*Papercutting Pattern Book*

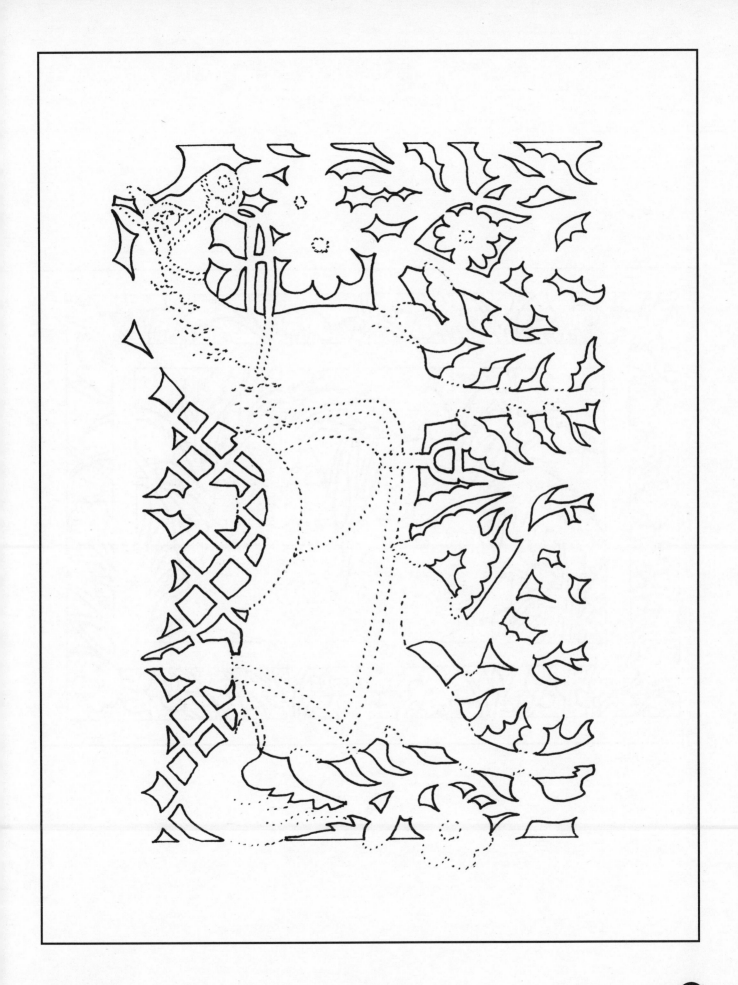

# Country Children

*Papercutting Pattern Book*

# Nautical

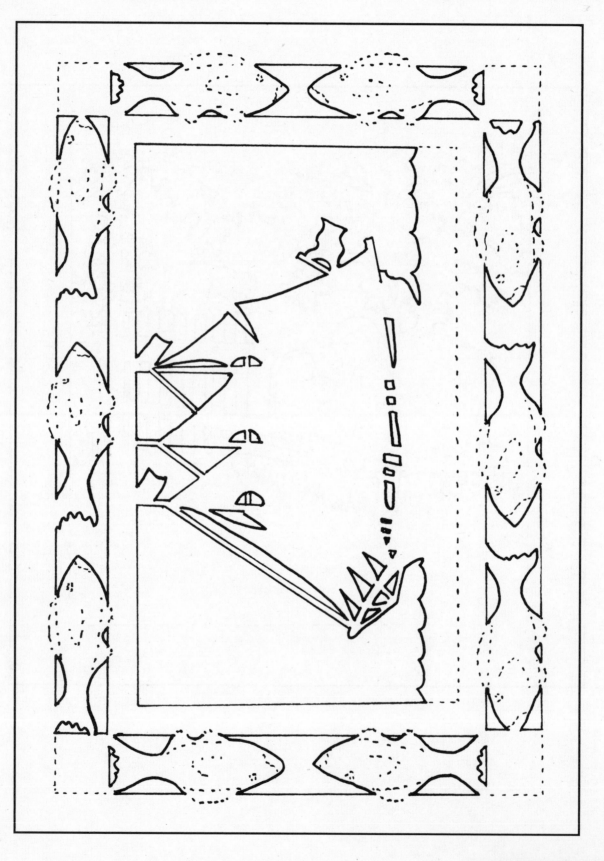

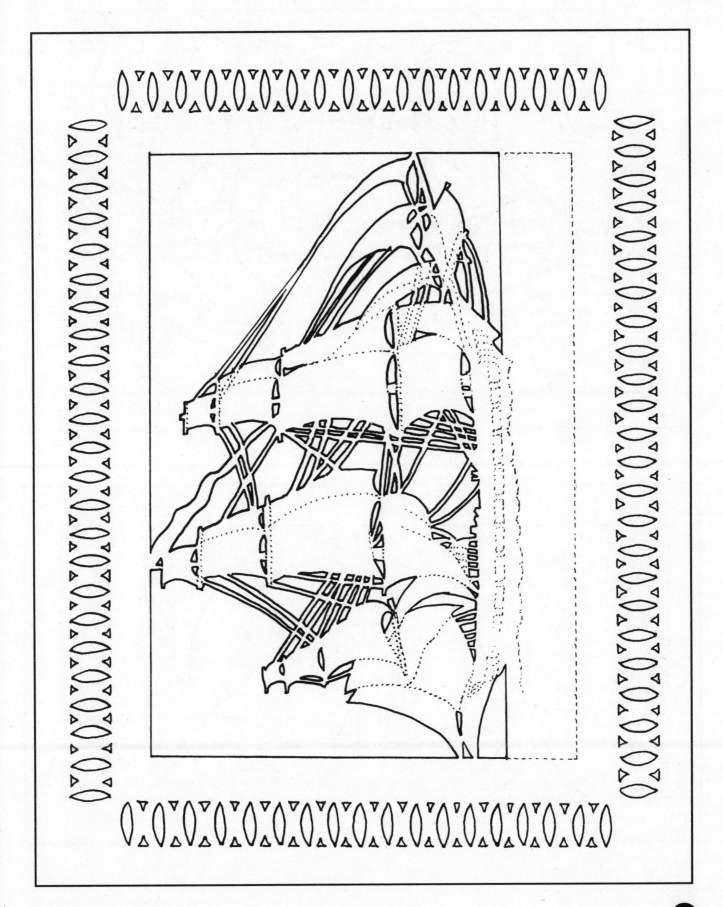

# *Pennsylvania Dutch Inspired*

*Papercutting Pattern Book*

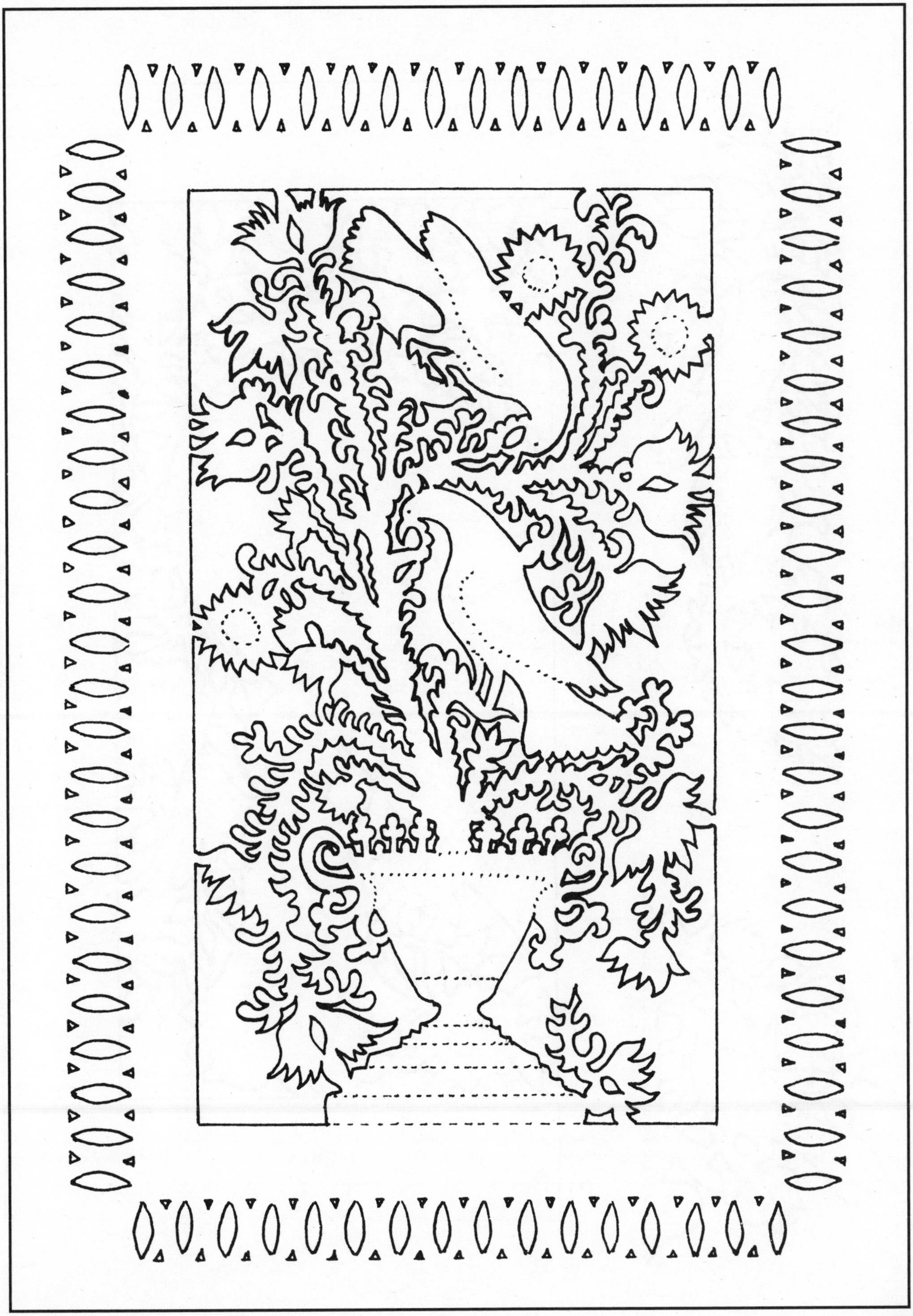

# Shaker Inspired

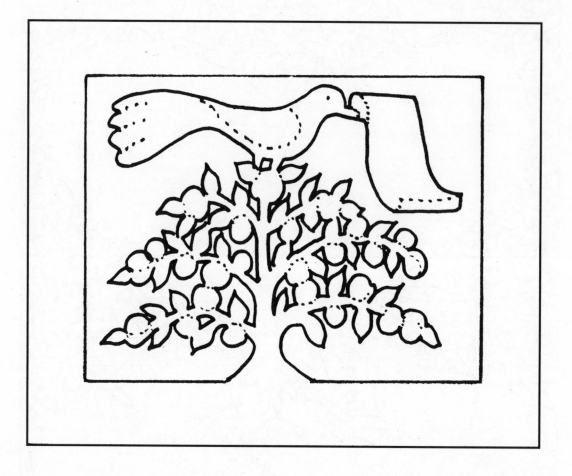

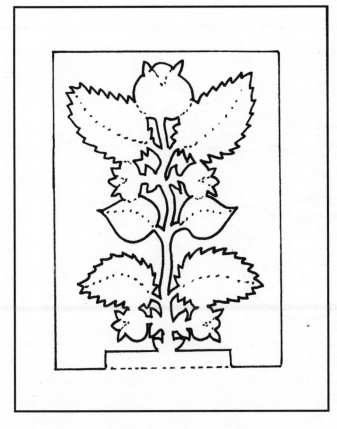

# Polish Inspired

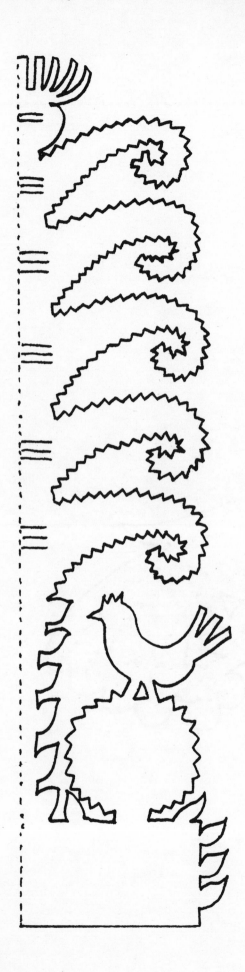

*Papercutting Pattern Book*

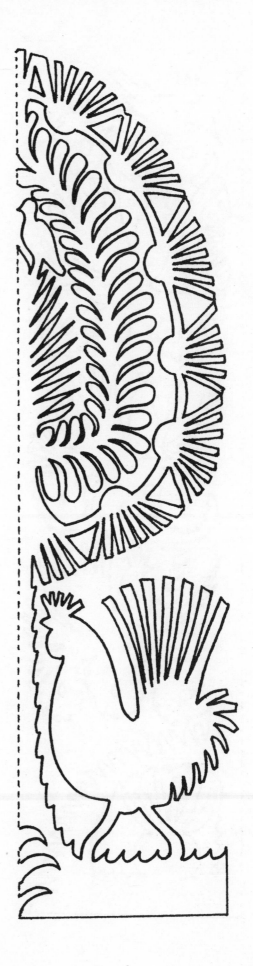

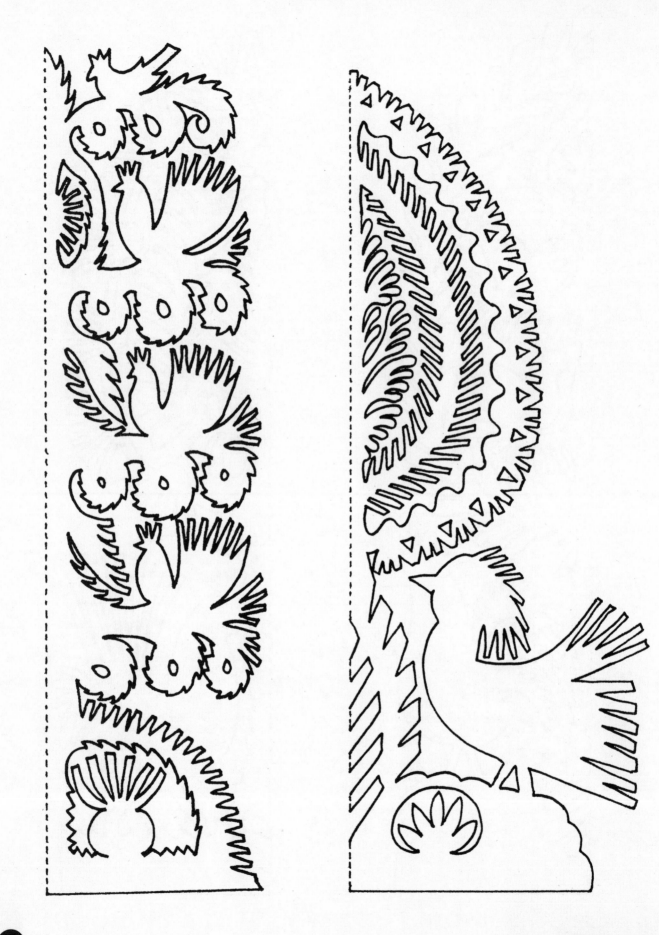

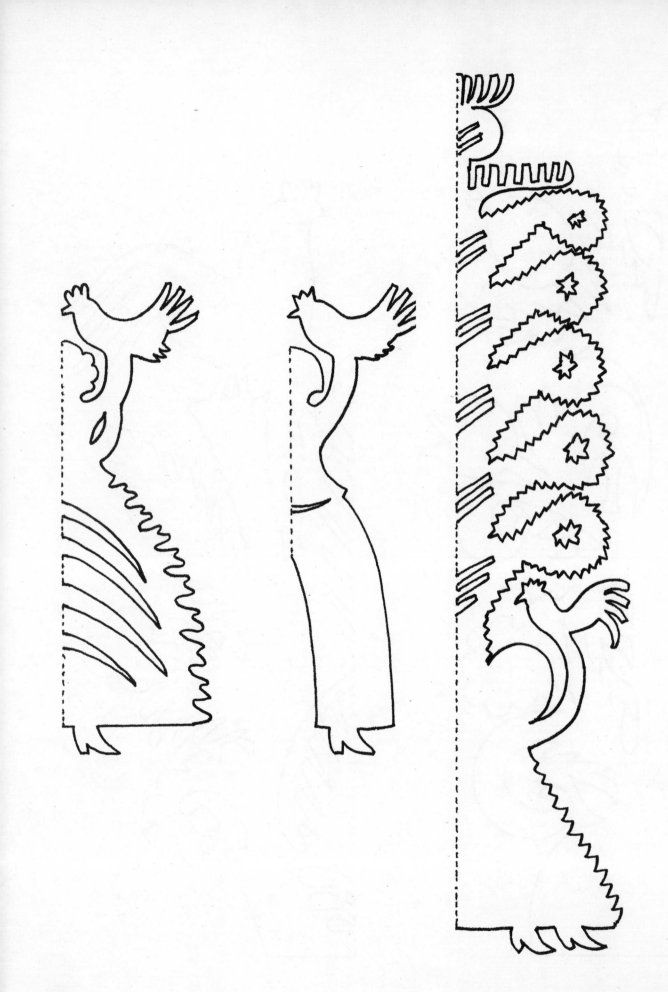

# Chinese Inspired

# Calendar

**Winter and Autumn, Summer and Spring**

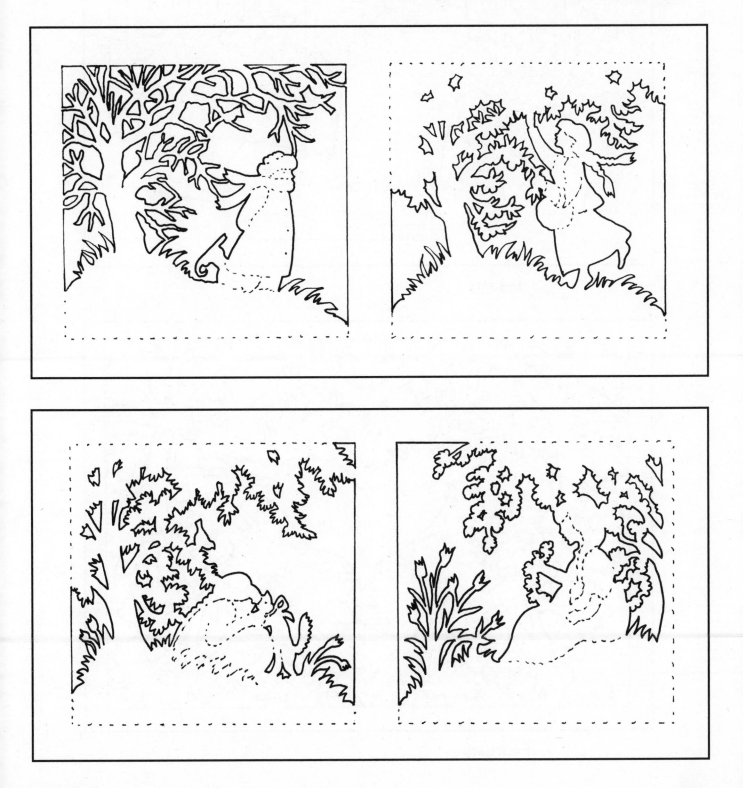

**January**

**February**

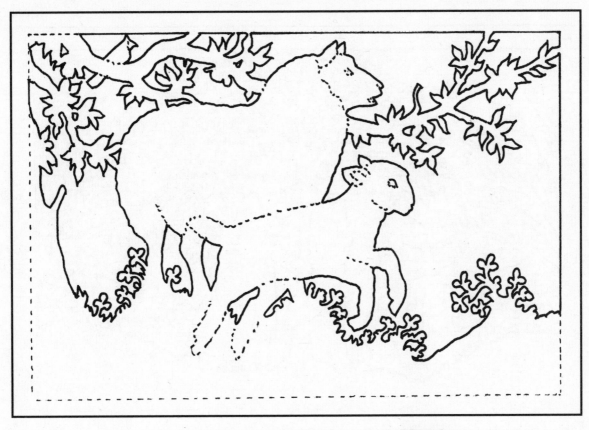

**March**

**April**

**May**

**June**

**July**

**August**

**September**

**October**

*Papercutting Pattern Book*

**November**

**December**

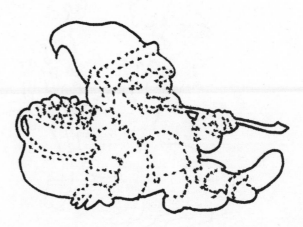

*Papercutting Pattern Book*

*Papercutting Pattern Book*

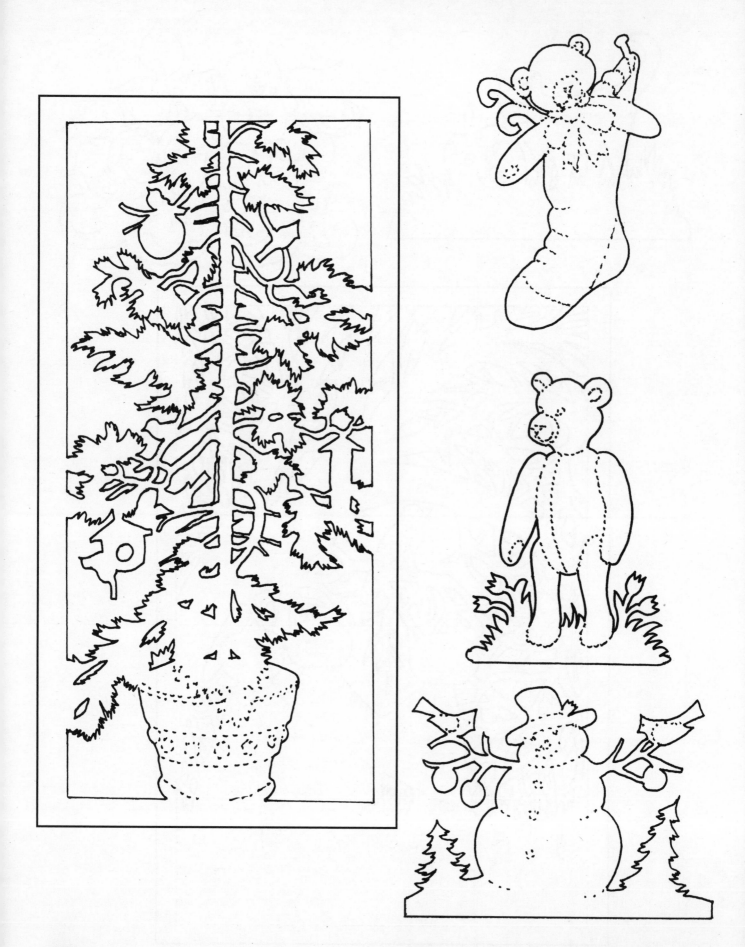

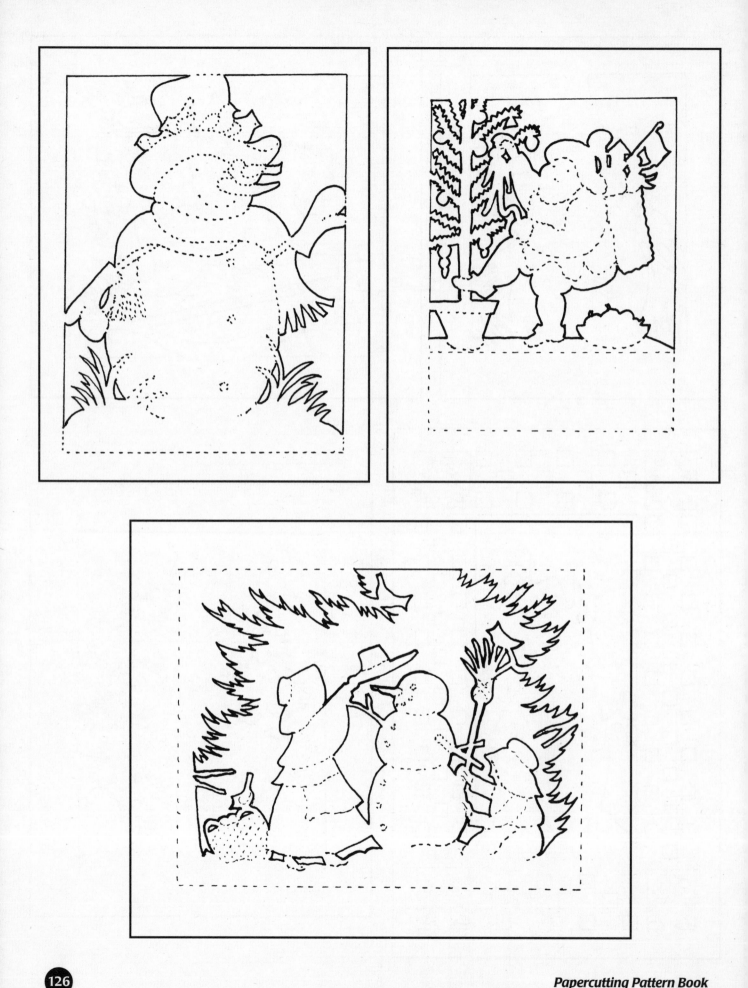

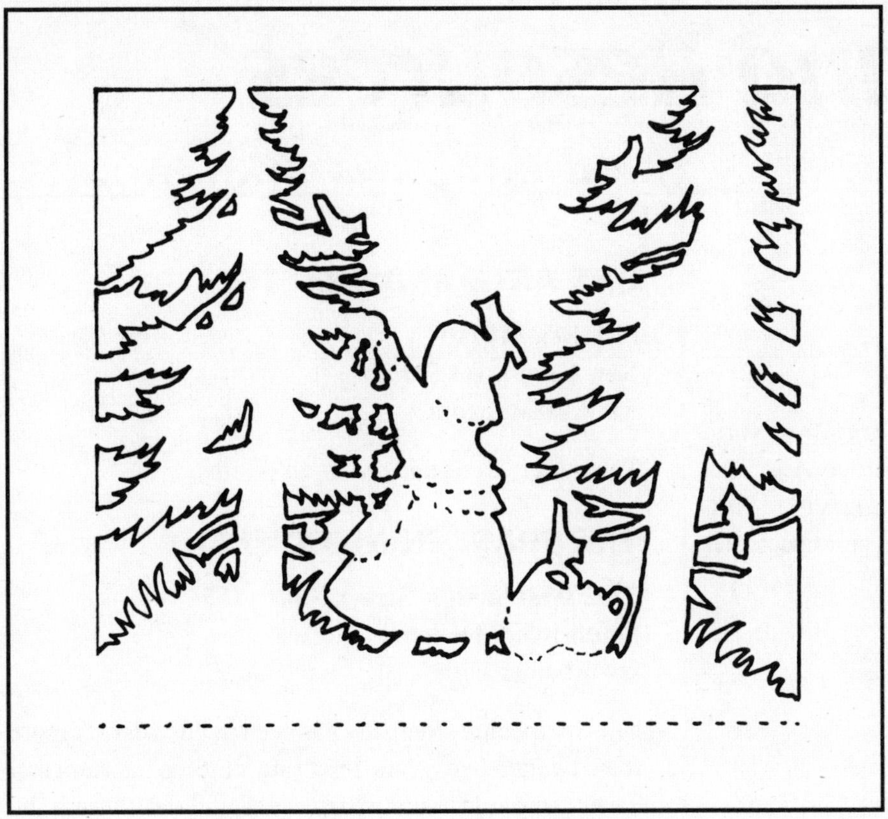

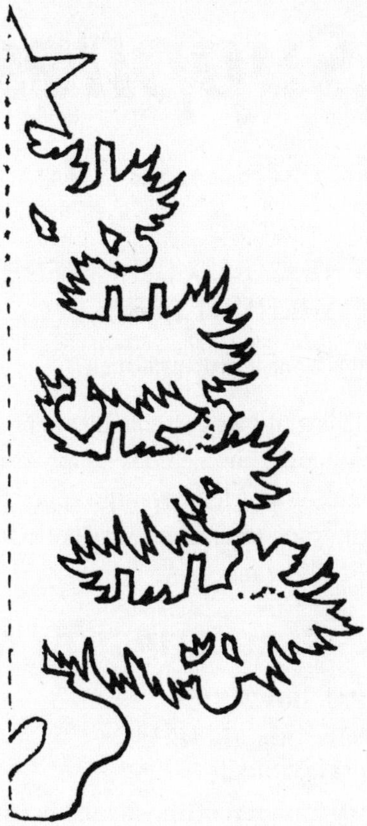

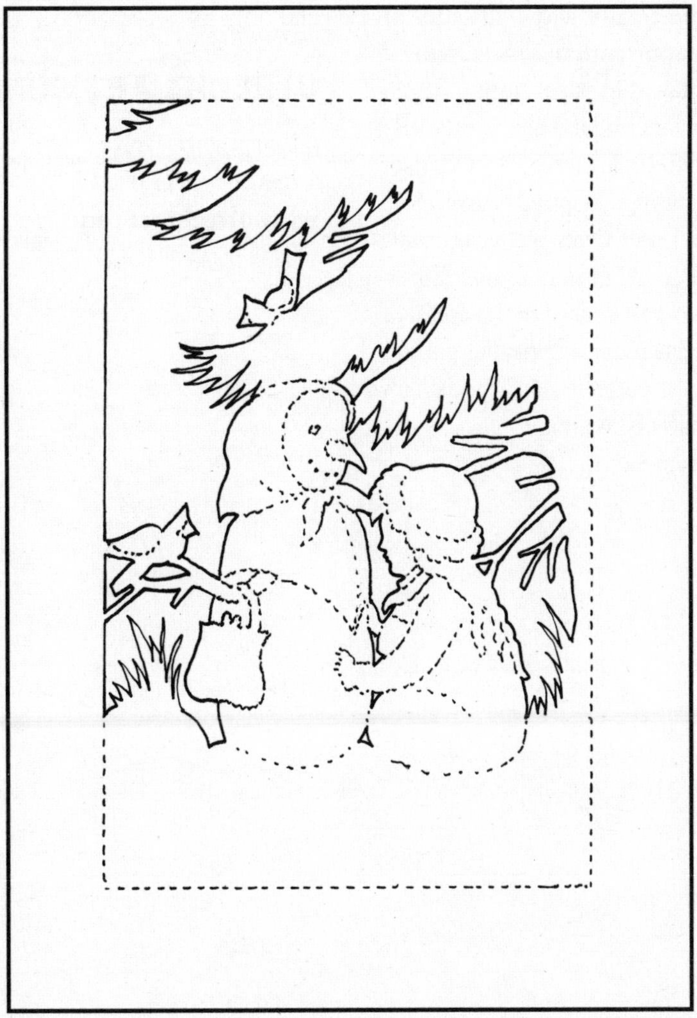

# Supplies and Resources

## THE GUILD OF AMERICAN PAPERCUTTERS

www.papercutters.org

This guild was established to promote the craft in North America, but includes members from Europe, Australia, and Asia. Membership ranges from beginners to full-time artists, teachers, and collectors. The guild publishes *First Cut* magazine quarterly.

## PAPERCUTTINGS BY ALISON

P.O. Box 2771
Sarasota, FL 34230
(941) 378-8411
www.papercuttingsbyalison.com

Papercuttings by Alison is the creator and distributor of the largest variety of papercutting patterns and supplies. Alison Cosgrove Tanner's interest in papercutting began in 1966 when she was nine years old and her family visited the home of Hans Christian Andersen in Odense, Denmark. Andersen's papercuttings inspired Alison. She started her own business in 1984. Over the years, Alison's husband, Chuck Tanner, and her mother and father, Gloria and Don Cosgrove, have all shared in the creative art and work together in the business, supplying cutters with scissors, various papers, patterns, and books on papercutting. An annual catalog is available.

## SAX ARTS AND CRAFTS

P.O. Box 510710
New Berlin, WI 53151
www.saxarts.com

They offer "everything your art desires."

## THE SHARPENING COMPANY

3702 West Sample Street, Suite 1105
South Bend, IN 46619
www.tsharp.com

The Sharpening Company has been in business for more than twenty-five years repairing cutting instruments. They can produce ultrasharp edges without altering the original design of the blade. Minimal metal is removed, and only as necessary.

## UTRECHT ART SUPPLIES

6 Corporate Drive
Cranbury, NJ 08512
www.utrechtart.com